ABOUT THE AUTHOR

Sean Wai Keung is a Glasgow-based poet and performer. His pamphlet *you are mistaken* won the Rialto Open Pamphlet Competition 2016 and he has also released *how to cook* and *be happy*, both with Speculative Books. He has developed solo performances with the National Theatre of Scotland, where he was a Starter Artist in 2017, Anatomy Arts, Magnetic North and the Fringe of Colour, and is also a poetry editor at EX/POST magazine. He holds degrees from Roehampton University, London, and the University of East Anglia, Norwich and has been published in *404Ink, Blood Bath, datableedzine* and *The Suburban Review*, amongst others. Full credits can be found at seanwaikeung.carrd.co

Instagram: @seanwaikeung
Twitter: @SeanWaiKeung

'One example of the "sociology of everyday communism", according to David Graeber, is "the familiar principle, common in both Europe and the Middle East, that those who have shared bread and salt must never harm one another". On one level, Sean Wai Keung's sikfan glaschu is a book about food, e.g. kfc, jumbo tapas, kfc again, pizza hut, xiaolongbao. On another, it's a book about what it means to share food. Eating together represents the utopian hope of Graeber's "everyday communism" – made more apparent in the self-isolated world of the pandemic – as well as delineating the boundaries of harm, in the context of endemic racism, "dodgy landlords", and a degrading service economy. Keung is aware of the cultural essentialism perpetrated by a kind of food fetishism ("chinese food doesnt really exist as a thing"), at the same time as he revels in food's ability to bind communities: "this place was built by migrants / therefore it is ours". Tonally, he treads a fine line between affectless melancholy and guileless sincerity, as when the speaker draws a pattern in coffee foam for a customer, "with the heart facing upwards / otherwise its bad luck / [it can look like a ballsack you see]" ('notes on coffee'). In other poems, he weaves together – or simply reproduces – restaurant reviews, wikipedia entries and online menus. This is a poetry collection as a collective of voices, mainly migrant voices living and working in Glasgow. The effect is of a poetics of care. Even when the speaker is most helpless – "the food banks are all empty and i cant look after anyone / the CB hotel sacked and evicted all their staff overnight and i cant look after anyone" – there's a baseline hope expressed in the inherent communalism of writing for others. Sharing food is both the metaphor and corollary. "i want to know what strong feelings it evokes in you to watch / your food being made rather than have it appear," writes Keung. And that's what sikfan glaschu does: these are poems that don't just appear pre-formed; they're made in front of you.' - *Will Harris*

sean wai keung
sikfan glaschu

VERVE
POETRY PRESS
BIRMINGHAM

PUBLISHED BY VERVE POETRY PRESS
https://vervepoetrypress.com
mail@vervepoetrypress.com

FIRST PUBLISHED APR 2021
REPRINTED MAY 2022

Printed and bound in the UK
by ImprintDigital, Exeter

ISBN: 978-1-912565-55-9

Cover photography by Karlie Wu 胡嘉瑤

For my 婆婆 *and* 公公. *With love.*

CONTENTS

fàilte gu glaschu

chinatown   11

star bar   12

di maggios   13

greggs   14

blue lagoon   15

sikfan glaschu   17

notes on coffee   18

calabash   22

brian maule at chardon d'or   24

willow tearooms   26

tinto tapas   27

ranjits kitchen   28

kfc central   29

baaibaai   30

rum shack   32

civic house   33

dumpling monkey   34

kurdish street food and shawarma   36

yadgar   37

paesano   39

topolabamba   41

tomb-sweeping day 2020 glaschu   42

pizza hut strathbungo   44

a lockdown changes everything/nothing

stay inside   46

kfc pollokshaws   49

the glad cafe   50

the chicken place   51

cafe wander   53

flying duck   55

conversations from the line outside the supermarket   56

falafel to go   58

the wee curry shop   59

wing rush   60

bloc   61

dreams from kitchens

where is the tree my 公公 drew   64

lanzhou noodle   66

byblos cafe   67

china sea   68

nandos   70

fusion palace   71

loon fung   72

yabbadabbadoo   74

time to go   76

Acknowledgements

sikfan glaschu

these poems were made during five years of eating and living in glaschu, scotland. they should not be taken as reviews – nor should the quality of the poems necessarily be seen to reflect on the quality of any food or place which may bare a similar name, in either a positive or negative light.

fàilte gu glaschu

chinatown

this place was built by migrants
therefore it is ours

they came from the gàidhealtachd
they came from the ghalltachd

       sometimes i wonder what my 公公 would have thought
       had he been given the chance to visit

       he had lived in other cities built by migrants
       hongkong – liverpool – bradford –

       i like to think that if he had been given the chance
       he would have liked it
       but who can know for sure

       when he first arrived in the uk i dont know
       what glaschu would have been like

chinatown here opened in 1992
the year after i was born

       i moved here three
       years after he died

this place was built by migrants
and we have been eating here ever since

star bar

a genuinely nice place and a staple of the stereotypically good
poor local diet – i mean its £3
for a three-course meal what isnt there
to love

you get soup
you get something with potatoes
                              [or mac and cheese]
you get jelly

***

while somewhere out beyond the faded bricks
the 38 speeds past with a busload of folk heading off
or on to jobs they may
love or hate but at least they have them
and for that price what else did you expect

di maggios

during your visit
when you turned to me and said *i promised them* [pointing
to them] *that glaschu has some amazing italian food*
and i looked at them and noticed all their hunger
and you continued *so i said to them that you would take us*
somewhere nice and you gave me that smile you gave me
sometimes [that same one from my childhood
that i hated]

what i said was *thats fine – we can go*
to di maggios but what i thought was something else
a sudden blurring of chakras or a flare up
of memories of shouting matches between us in italian restaurants
in cities far away [when they werent with you]
the comic-sans-esque font of a *spaghetti house* in tsim sha tsui
a disagreement over birthrights at a *carluccios* in stratford

and you [still giving me that smile] said *o – is that a good one then*

and i looked at them and noticed again
[that they were not there back then] their
[that none of this is their fault] hunger

and so i said *yes – it is* and i started to lead you down
buchanan street and all i kept thinking
was that this time it would be different
that this time there would be no fighting
that this city really does have amazing italian food
and that sometimes thats enough

greggs

one day some rando in the queue
tells me that what you order is dependant entirely on your
personality type

i asked them to explain so they did

> sausage roll – classy/elegant/no-nonsense
> steak bake – deep-thinking/complex/warm
> chicken bake – arsty/professional/lucky
> bean/cheese melt – fun/kinky/light-hearted
> beef pasty – morbid/energetic/hopeful
> pizza slice – always wanting to be in the middle of it all
> vegan sausage roll – cool/loving/life-affirming
> a sandwich – gentle/anxious/trusting
> salad or soup – mysterious/possibly untrustworthy

and as i placed my own order i found myself
thinking that maybe the rando was right

i mean whos to say where exactly it is
that these things really do come from

blue lagoon

"Italy and the fascist involvement in World War II brought many hardships on Italians settled in Scotland – many families were separated as adult males were interned. The family members that were left behind were forced to cope with mistrust and discrimination. Of those imprisoned many men found themselves held in Northern Ireland and the Isle of Man. A number of others were employed in Orkney, at Scapa Flow, to construct a barrier against Nazi U-boats. These men additionally constructed the Chapel of Lambholm from scrap metal and junk. Nowadays, this chapel is one of Orkney's most popular tourist attractions." [1]

In 1975 on Sauchiehall Street, Glaschu, the first Blue Lagoon Fish & Chip shop opened. Owned by Ersilio Varese, who had arrived in Scotland from Italy in 1965, and his wife Edda, the shop immediately proved a huge hit.

"Latest available figures from the 2011 UK census show there were 6,048 people born in Italy living in Scotland. This was up from 4,936 in 2001 and 3,947 recorded in 1991. Ronnie Convery, secretary of the Italian Scotland charitable organisation and director of communications at the Archdiocese of Glaschu, asserted that a completely new dimension was being added to the Scots-Italians community. He said, 'There has been a brand new migration over the past two years, and the biggest one we have seen in 100 years.' The majority come from the provinces of Lucca, Parma, Frosinone and Isernia." [1]

Today there are 12 franchised Blue Lagoon outlets. They are directed and ran by Ersilio and Edda's son Angelo and grandchildren Simone, Alessandro and Gianluca. Collectively they employ around 200 people.

1] Source: wikipedia.org/wiki/Italian-Scots

sikfan glaschu

the megabus got in late
about 7am
was supposed to be 6.30

it was a typically windy day
but i didnt know that then

this was going to be it
my new life in a new city
exciting

not knowing where i was
going i zombied into the nearest pret
[nothing else seemed open at the time]
where i ordered a filter coffee / croissant / banana

then sat by the window thinking about being a kid again
sitting in my room writing stupid rhymes for fun
hearing that familiar evening shout of *sikfan* meaning
your food is ready

as soon as i would leave my room i would smell it
freshly steamed rice or vegetables with oyster sauce
or a pie crisping up in the oven
                                    dont you miss that

the eagerness / the hunger / the sense of mystery
the not-knowing exactly what would be waiting on the table
but knowing that whatever it was
                                    it would be delicious

notes on coffee

1
heat milk before shots
this is important since
a cold coffee shot will
cause customers to be
come monsters with
ancient roaring voices
gunning to kill you or worse
get you fired

2
always upsell the special blend
these are the words you should use

it has a stronger taste
it is smoother
it will create more positive energy in your pineal glands
which will seep out into the world
in the form of benevolent thoughts

do not mention the extra price
unless they ask
in which case tell them but also tell them that its worth it
because it is

3
a heart is an acceptable and easy pattern to craft
on the top of a flat white
however if choosing to flex your individuality
by applying the heart pattern
always give the customer their drink
with the heart facing upwards
otherwise its bad luck
[it can look like a ballsack you see]

alternatively you may always choose
one of the other approved patterns instead
such as a flower

4
one yellow tag on jug equals soy milk
two yellow tags on jug equals coconut milk
brown tag on jug equals almond milk
white tag on jug equals lactofree milk
purple tag on jug equals oat milk
red tag on jug equals skimmed milk
blue tag on jug equals whole milk
green tag on jug equals semi-skimmed milk
no tag on jug equals chocolate
an infinity of tags on jug equals

5
always talk to them
they must know you
are friendly and loving
your life here at the coffee shop

                                    which you are

6

the regulars will be allowed
to ask you where you are from
and to know what gender you are
and to know your name

they are the lifeblood of you and as such they shall be respected

7

you must be present at minimum five minutes
before your shift begins
failure to do so will result in penalties
such as one more year being added to your lifespan
which you will have to spend here

8

any and all training will be done in your own time
this will include learning how to be a better person
as well as how to get away with not paying your rent on time

9

once you have achieved the prestigious position of master
barista you will

10

for you this will just be another coffee
another minute during another shift
on another day in another week

for them this could be their one social interaction of the day
their coffee could make the difference between a good day
or a bad day
maybe they will meet someone in the street
an old flame perhaps
and because of the coffee that you have given them
perhaps they will have the energy to engage in polite conversation

perhaps during this conversation they will realise that they both share
the same taste for coffee
perhaps they will realise that they are both regulars
in your shop

perhaps this coincidence will reignite their interest in each other
and they will agree to purchase their next coffees here
together

after a few times doing this maybe they will start officially dating
then after a while they will be blessed with their own accommodation

and perhaps their rent will always be paid on time
and perhaps they will be forever happy
and perhaps this will all have been
because of you

calabash

1

after twenty minutes of trying
to decide we eventually just went
for the jumbo tapas option
which contained a portion of ugali
mukimo plantain coconut rice
nyama choma kuku choma keema
curry boerewors w/ bbq dip
and kachumbari

2

there was football on the tv
behind where i was sitting and i
told you to not tell me anything
as i wanted to watch the game
on catchup later but still i couldnt
help but hear the occasional sound
of cheers or shouts from both the
tv screen and the other customers

3

when the food did come out we agreed
that it was beautiful and that we must take
photos of it before we tasted it
and so we did and in truth i have
not shown those photos to a
single soul in the time since
although i do sometimes look at
them when im sitting in on my own

4

when i eventually watched the game
later that night it turned out to be so
boring that i nodded off and fell asleep
in front of it which struck me
as strange since i had heard all that
cheering etc. and to this day i still have
no idea what any of that was about but

5

hey at least the ugali was
beautiful

brian maule at chardon d'or

i had the crisp ox tongue w/ charred shallots and caper herb jus

you had the creamed goats cheese w/ pickled beetroot and candied walnuts

i had the grilled sea bream w/ fricassee of white beans and pancetta and baby leeks

you had the pan fried stone bass w/ spiced puree and roast cauliflower and kale

i had the crème brûlée flavoured w/ vanilla

you had the extra bitter dark chocolate mousse w/ griottine cherries and curd

we talked about the concept of warm-and-cold in chinese medicine and cooking
we talked about the gàidhlig language and highland migration and traditions
we talked about poetry and registering as self-employed
we talked about the norwegian community of dumfries

24

this all happened on the same day that michel roux died

we asked the maître d' if he would consider the restaurant to be french or scottish
as different food review lists named it in different categories

he said it was scottish food cooked using french techniques

when we went to shake his hand he pulled away and said we arent allowed
to do that any more

we both said sorry
we forgot
and then we went
to get the train home

willow tearooms

if big charles could make it here then so can we
he came all the way from the ceann a' bhaile to the postcards
selling in the tourist shops for £1
a legacy spanning an entire city
- and now it could be our turn to take it for ourselves

        cnoc a' ghobhainn

                                 coille challtainn

the gorbals

                 merchant city

          we could replace them all with our own designs
just imagine it

       walking through dennistoun or pàrtaig and seeing
our names there instead

street names reworked to feature our different identities
instead of triangle trade merchants or whatever

pàirc na banrìghinn would become pàirc na imrich
allt an fhuairainn would become allt an dhaoine

and everywhere we looked we would own

---

ceann a' bhaile = townhead
cnoc a' ghobhainn = govanhill
coille challtainn = cowcaddens
the gorbals = the gorbals
merchant city = merchant city
dennistoun = dennistoun

pàrtaig = partick
pàirc na banrìghinn = queens park
pàirc na imrich = migrants park
allt an fhuairainn = springburn
allt an dhaoine = peoples stream

tinto tapas

sometimes i have thoughts like *i wish*
i knew more about spanish food and then i wonder
if thinking like that is culturally insensitive
especially since im always telling people
that chinese food doesnt really exist as a thing
in the same way that british food doesnt really exist
as a thing and maybe thats the same with spanish
food in fact i know it probably is yet somehow
my brain is still stuck in that way of thinking
as if things should always be defined so broadly
like yes ok so british food consists of lots of different
cuisines but at the same time if you say a sunday roast
most people would know you meant a british sunday roast
in the same way that if you said fan most people would know
that you meant *chinese* fan but anyway all im saying is
ive never eaten spanish food that i havent liked
and im sorry that i dont know more about it

ranjits kitchen

/ give me a barfi made from ancestor-memories
a lassi sweetened with mango
the daal of the day
a handful of pakora
a thali
and an irn bru

in return next time i come i promise to bring
all my friends to you
and we will huddle in a corner together
while the snow falls outside
order panjabi tea
and write you helpful yelp reviews
or poems made collaboratively
with our wide open mouths /

kfc central

the techno bin man is at it again scaring the tourist folk
and boring the locals but in here we are safe
nestled in our own corner-seats
our plastic trays perfectly aligned
mouths full of it

nobody can scare us here
or bore us

its just us
and our whole lives ahead of us
living our best

[w/ gravy on the side]

baaibaai

in hongkong cantonese *baaibaai* is how you informally say goodbye
having never gone to chinese school i cant remember
how i know this

i only went to english school
which means that the only language i know is english

currently im learning gàidhlig
it just seemed suddenly interesting to me one day
despite – or perhaps because of – the current limited number
of practical applications for the language
after all i dont know anyone who only speaks gàidhlig
without english

in gàidhlig to say goodbye you could say *mar sin leibh*
or *mar sin leat*
or the more informal *tioraidh*
which one you use is partly-determined by your social status
in relation with who you are saying goodbye to

the last time i was in hongkong i made a real effort
to say *baaibaai* to everyone there i knew i wouldnt see again
for a long time

in a bar near the mong kok mtr station they were playing
Goodbye's [The Saddest Word] by céline dion
i dont think i had heard it before
but right there in the bar it moved me

one of the first things i learned in gàidhlig is how to say
where i am from – *tha mi à place-name*

in order to practice this i of course had to pick a place i was from
i started off with *tha mi à glaschu* for *i am from glaschu*
which is where i live

then i went with *tha mi à sasainn* for *i am from england*
which is where i was born

then *tha mi à hongkong*

Goodbye's [The Saddest Word] by céline dion ends with the lyrics
"'Til we meet again / Until then / Goodbye"
which seems to imply that her version of a goodbye is not
a forever goodbye
more of a see you soon
or *tìoraidh an-dràsta*

i like this version of goodbye the best

especially the way céline dion says it
it makes me really believe it

when i tried to speak hongkong cantonese in hongkong
people spoke english back to me instead
clearly understanding
how inept i was

since that trip i havent learned any more
hongkong cantonese although
i am enjoying gàidhlig instead

and while it does feel like i havent been back
to where im from in years now
perhaps its for the best

rum shack

still dont fully know what brought me here [to
glaschu i mean] i just felt some kind of magnetic pull
almost as if i had no choice

in a good way for instance i still remember
the first time we both came here [to southside i mean]
which both of us had previously been warned about
from people we had met who had moved away

from here yet when we walked through [southside i mean]
down viccy road past the world food shops
and through the parks and tenement-lined roads
and by the train stations and through shawlands
and pollokshields and further along we both agreed

that we felt something good here – it seemed like a decent part
of town – and we went to the glad cafe and ordered
a coffee and talked to someone who recommended that
we give the rum shack a try
and when we did give it a try [the rum shack

i mean] we both agreed that our futures here seemed bright
and now its years later and i still live here but you dont
and the glad got redecorated and viccy road redeveloped
but the tenements still stand and so does the rum shack
and i still dont know why i came here [but here i am] [and
i am mostly happy here] [and i hope that wherever you are now
you are mostly happy too]

civic house

KITCHEN

Civic House Kitchen is a public canteen for Speirs Locks.

It's open over lunchtimes, serving a single dish cooked on the day.

A simple format allows the chefs to put time and effort into the food but still keep the price low.

Lunch costs £5 and refillable teas and coffees are £1.50. Check our daily dish on our Instagram OR just drop in.

All the food served is vegan [without meat, fish, eggs or dairy.]

OPENING HOURS: TUES-FRI 10am – 4pm

dumpling monkey

when she mentions *dumpling*
monkey and says that its *the best chinese in glaschu* you think immediately
of years ago and meeting up in town [not this town a different town] with
your mum who you had agreed to go to lunch with and so you went to the market
and there was a van selling dumplings – you could have them fried or steamed
in batches of six or ten or twelve – and you both decided to share six of each
and when your mum went up to order from the van the guy started to talk
in mandarin which neither of you could speak and so she just repeated her order
in english again which seemed to confuse the poor guy but he still started making them
and minutes later you and your mum took your freshly fried/steamed dumplings
and went to sit together on that wall near the anglican church at the far end
of the market and you shared your dumplings and you dont remember what
you talked about but you do remember they tasted good

then when you eventually go to *the best chinese*
in glaschu and you see on their menu that they do congee you immediately forget
about memories of eating dumplings and instead you think about being a kid again
in an airport early in the morning feeling sleepy from jumping time zones
and you ordered a big bowl of congee with a couple of youtiao and before then
your only experience of congee had been homemade congee
you had never thought it would be something that you could just order somewhere
so you ate it and it was so different from what you had eaten in the past
when your mum or your 婆婆 had made it for you but it was still really nice
– just different – and just the knowledge that it was possible
to order congee for breakfast in certain places in the world really
did make you feel more at ease with being alive

Then when you call your mum and tell her
that youve been to *the best chinese in glaschu*
and she asks you what you ate and you tell her congee and she asks if it was nice
you will say that it was fine and you will open up and say that you miss her
cooking and she will tell you that you shouldnt have moved away then
and it hurts a bit but you know that at least shes saying it with love

kurdish street food and shawarma

its simple really you only get a handful of choices here
    chicken or lamb
    wrap or flatbread
    salad
    sauce
    a drink maybe

  and then you wait

        [seriously though
this place is so fucking delicious you have to give it a try just trust me]

yadgar

1] choose the window seat in the corner because that way you can always keep track of everything else thats happening in the room – just in case

2] wonder if its a table-service-place or a go-to-the-counter place

3] one of you orders the veg the other orders the meat

4] a few blocks away people are threatened with eviction from their tenements because they dont have electricity and arent safe to live in but where else will they go

5] talk about your new projects even if the other doesnt ask but still remember that this is all fine

6] dont fuck this up sean

7] rice or bread or both or none make the choice

8] wonder how to spell yadgar correctly

9] monitor what other people eat as well to see what looks good for next time

10] listen to shouting in another language from behind the door but remain calm as its not angry shouting just normal shouting

11] dont mention the burn marks stinging on either of your chests

12] discuss the flavour profile and the feelings and memories that each dish evokes

13] accidentally order some kind of raita thinking its a sweet then laugh at the mistake while also feeling guilty for not already knowing what things are

14] walk back part of the way together

15] tell each other what a great night its been

16] hug

17] thats it

paesano

we will be together there and we will eat italian food and it will
    be brilliant

saremo insieme e mangeremo cibo italiano e sarà geniale

bidh sinn còmhla an-sin agus ithidh sinn biadh eadailteach agus
    bidh e sgoinneil

you are invited too

anche tu sei invitato

gheibh thu cuireadh cuideachd

glaschu will be our mother

glaschu sarà nostra madre

bidh glaschu mar mhàthair dhuinn

our father will be somewhere else

nostro padre sarà da qualche altra parte

bidh ar n-athair am badeigin eile

and will speak another language

e parlerà un'altra lingua

agus bruidhnidh e cànan eile

to his good health!

alla sua buona salute!

a shlàinte mhath!

topolabamba

dear mexico
how are you today
hope your spirits are up despite everything thats been going on lately
whats the weather like over there at the moment
its been pretty sunny for the most part here which is a bit different
although the news says the rain will come back again soon enough

once this has all blown over you should definitely come visit
i would offer to come there myself but lets face it
you would probably prefer it here
you could even stay with us while youre over if you like
we could share war stories over a dram
play a few rounds of scrabble or write an exquisite corpse together

ive noticed you managing to stay pretty active recently
not that i stalk you on social media or anything of course
although i must admit that whenever you post a food pic
i find myself uncontrollably salivating

everything just looks so fucking tasty you see
and when i see something tasty i want it

so hurry on over as soon as you can
ok

o and remember to keep smiling
whatever happens

tomb-sweeping day 2020 glaschu

with thoughts of my 婆婆 and 公公 in england

i tried to imagine once what it would be like
living over half your life without being fluent
in the local language – how much more intelligent
you would have to become at things such as social
cues and body language – at reading expressions
more times correctly than
incorrectly – if you failed then the consequences could be

***

all my life i thought i had a slick imagination for that sort
of thing – even as a kid i would flick through the world
atlas looking up faraway places and think about what
life may be like over there
what kind of food they might eat
what language they might speak
if there would be anyone there who looked like me

***

meanwhile down the road at the front desk of the spring
bamboo they would sit together at the same time everyday
in a calm silence
thinking about inconsequential things
but doing so 客家話

and there would be no need for words

because she knew that he had already put the change in the till
and he knew that she had already flicked the switch on the fryers
from the circle diagram to the one-line diagram
and they both knew that in a few minutes time they would unlock
the front door together before flipping the plastic sign
from the red side reading *closed*
to the blue one reading *open*

pizza hut strathbungo

despite the rain
despite the mess of public transport
despite the history of religious tension
despite the wind
despite the low life expectancy
despite the links to british colonialism
despite the ever-increasing rents
despite the hipsters and students
despite the drug and drink problems
despite the corrupt politicians
despite the crumbling tenements
despite the racism
despite the smell of sewage and breweries
despite the littering
despite the vast economic differences between areas
despite the motorway in the middle of it all
despite the cold cold winters
despite the claustrophobic subway
despite the munchy box meals for one
despite the 10pm alcohol curfew
despite the banker wankers
despite the pollution
despite the dodgy landlords
despite the isolation
despite the potholes
despite the pigeons
despite it all
im still so glad to be here

a lockdown changes everything/nothing

stay inside

everyone is being told to stay in their houses and i cant look after anyone

the hospitals are all too full and i cant look after anyone

my friends are scattered all over the world and i cant look after anyone

the nurses are roaming empty supermarket aisles and i cant look after anyone

i am having fever dreams about my own death and i cant look after anyone

old gentle AH is no longer allowed in his regular cafe and i cant look after anyone

thousands have died in china and i cant look after anyone

zines are asking for poetry submissions and i cant look after anyone

AL is coughing again and i cant look after anyone

the internet is full of memes about it and i cant look after anyone

a politician shakes hands with another and i cant look after anyone

all the pubs are closed and i cant look after anyone

theres shouting from the building across from mine and i cant look after anyone

ive yet to hear from AS and i cant look after anyone

BC is in her second shop today looking for toilet paper and i cant look after anyone

all the festivals have been cancelled and i cant look after anyone

the new kfc manager is being pressured to keep her shop open and i cant look after anyone my mum messages me to say shes feeling so low and i cant look after anyone

someone claims they have the cure–all they need is money first and i cant look after anyone

FH has to self-isolate with a partner she fears and i cant look after anyone

everyones confused as to when the bins will get taken out and i cant look after anyone

all the phonelines are busy and i cant look after anyone

my 婆婆 is all on her own and i cant look after anyone

i dont know if antidepressants count as high priority medication and i cant look after anyone

BTs book launch has to be cancelled and i cant look after anyone

the news is filled with nothing else and i cant look after anyone

LS says her work may have to lay her off and i cant look after anyone

the football season has been postponed and i cant look after anyone

nobody is buying my poetry and i cant look after anyone

TG is so anxious she can only eat if shes drunk and i cant look after anyone

the highlands have told people to stay away and i cant look after anyone

all the podcasts are begging people to sign up to their patreons and i cant look after anyone

this house is not big enough for the all of us and i cant look after anyone

there are still sirens even though the streets are empty and i cant look after anyone

DD thinks shes got it and i cant look after anyone

the food banks are all empty and i cant look after anyone

the CB hotel sacked and evicted all their staff overnight and i cant look after anyone

PV cant get her money back from the yoga retreat she had to cancel and i cant look after anyone

theres a pain in my chest and i cant look after anyone
youre a thousand miles away from here and i cant look after anyone
yet still i cant stop myself from thinking of you
but i cant look after anyone

kfc pollokshaws

as the virus tears through glaschu i sit
my googlemaps open on *kentucky* wondering how
the chicken tastes over there or
how essential their workers may or may not be

earlier i was looking through menus
seeing what was open/closed locally [without
going outside of course] but it started me off
thinking about a time i previously met you
on a snowy grey afternoon after i got off
my morning shift up at the coffee shop
i didnt order anything
but you had a box-meal-for-one
after you finished we went home and i cooked
for myself

what a memory

as far as i can tell the internet is insufficient
at encapsulating what *kentucky* really means
– its just a far-off blob i cant fathom
a mass of essential people i cant know
living their lives
getting on with things
like chickens sometimes do

the glad cafe

one day i decide to rearrange my room
to see if a change in surroundings makes me feel anything
different so my bed goes slightly to the left
so that the chair i took from the library
[back when the library was being refurnished
and asked people to rehome their old furniture] fits
in the space to the right of my bed and my coffee table
that i took from my old flat [back when i moved out
and asked the landlord if i could take it with me
and she said sure] then goes to the left so that its
perpendicular to the small desk that you gave me back when you
were here and which i rarely use apart from when i zoom people
partly because ive never had a desk before so im not in the habit
of using one and partly because when i look at it i do think of you
and what it was like back when you were still around
and maybe because of this its always struck me as the perfect place
to put small things that remind me of you like a sea shell
or other small things that remind me of other people
like an empty bottle of beirão or a small owl figurine
and lets face it having such items on a desk is not conducive
to sitting at said desk and getting important things [like emails]
or boring things [like paying council tax] done but hey tomorrow
is a new day and once the rearrangement is finally complete
who knows what will happen and i wish you were here
because then i could say to you that i really dont need
this desk and that you should probably just keep it for yourself
and that while i do like the idea of sitting at it and writing you letters
we both know that all it will really do is clutter
the place up o and also i miss you and thank you so much
for everything

the chicken place

21/04/2020 – 4 ½ stars – The food was good with generous portions as usual. The food was warm which is the norm from the place. The corn was not provided though. Understandably under the conditions the delivery was slightly late.

21/04/2020 – 5 stars – Chicken Chicken bucket was great, but the chips were soggy and unseasoned.

20/04/2020 – 4 ½ stars – Food was tasty but pretty cold on arrival, wouldn't call what I got popcorn chicken either but delivery was quick!

20/04/2020 – 3 stars – Food was alright slightly cool but luke warm enough to eat it. Forgot inferno bites from my order which I paid for. Not bothering the restaurant over the sake of a 2 quid item and the hour wait for it to be sorted.

20/04/2020 – 6 stars – Amazing will definitely be back

20/04/2020 – 3 stars – Orded the spicey burger come cold would like a free meal cos it was all cold

19/04/2020 – 5 stars – Extremely dry chicken pieces. My little boy couldn't chew them. Even I couldn't eat them. Peri peri chicken, however, was nice and soft.

19/04/2020 – 6 stars – Thanks it was lovely jubbly

19/04/2020 – 1 star – [no comment left]

16/04/2020 – 5 ½ star – Very pleased with the nice food and speedy service. Thanks, would definitely order again.

16/04/2020 – 1 ½ star – The main thing that was okay was hot shots though not so "hot" like my sister's last order. Chips were soggy and peri peri strips were tiny think and dry with no taste at all as i thought marinade would be same as peri peri whole chicken but nope the whole peri peri chicken was so dry slight burnt and had zero marinade unlike 2 weeks or so when sister order same thing. All is all had high expectation but was very disappointed as was good not so long ago :[

16/04/2020 – 4 star – [no comment left]

16/04/2020 – 1 ½ star – Didn't get my food ?????

cafe wander

daily walk starting point: queens park over by the glad cafe and di maggios

then through queens park to viccy road govanhill side

down viccy road til that weird bit by star bar where it kinda splits in two

take the pollokshaws road split

walk down under the m74 right to the end where you should see the brazen head
[you cant miss it its the one thats always in celtic colours]

turn left and follow the arches up gorbals street past the citz

you will get to a junction by the big central mosque – keep following the road upwards

walk over the bridge o look theres the clyde

walk through town a bit see that nothing is open then go back to that bridge

walk past the clutha before following clyde street til you get
to the green

walk through the green taking the most southerly path following the river

keep going til you get to the suspension bridge go on walk over it why not eh

follow the path up through the weird residential bit til you get to the big road

turn a right if you pass the strath
clyde distillery then you are going the right way

once you walk far enough you will get to the junction near the central mosque and the citz again

take a left and head back the same way you got here

flying duck

at some point i realised i had seen more of the ducks
in the park than i had of any single human being

i had even started to recognise a few of them
[or at least thought that i recognised them] the one with the big

white spot on his face for instance or the other who always seemed
to be sitting beyond the pond somewhere by the trees without

a care in the world and who i took to calling mo because that was
the sound he seemed to make whereas other ducks made more

of a regular *kqwak* kind of sound mo would definitely make a
mo kind of sound but then again what if thats a sound

that all ducks make – what if all this time mo hasnt been one
single duck but a series of ducks all sitting in similar places

making similar sounds what if there are many ducks with white spots
on their faces and i just never realised it

what if they recognised every day that i was on my way over
and they kqwaked at each other to get into positions

you be mo this time one would say
but i was mo yesterday would come the reply

then they would smack their webbed feet into position
and wait for my inevitable arrival

conversations from the line outside the supermarket

isnt this terrible

my husband is waiting in the car

i thought it would be quieter today

dont i know you from somewhere

last time round they still didnt have toilet roll

im trying to stock up

can you believe this

no way this is two meters

its the children i feel most for

im shopping for her too

at least the suns out eh

i heard theres a cure on its way mind

you cant trust what any of them say

what have you been cooking then

is this the right queue surely not

its just a conspiracy see

this is my third attempt today

i just hope its over soon

i was already standing here

im starting to lose track of the days

my daughters working in there

its one rule for them and another for us

theres no flour anywhere

have you talked to anyone else recently

is it just one of us that can go in then

youre wearing your mask wrong

its a time of crisis – they should prioritise people like us before others

ive been told to get rosé but i got no clue

in india they have it worse

they had some in the worldfood shop yesterday

you know what i havent talked to another person all day

please dont talk to me

its so stupid that everyone is panic buying

this will only last another week

i cant be arsed with this

whats on your shopping list

am i safe to go in now

sorry

you must be loving this

thank you

have a good one

falafel to go

even before the virus there were takeaway only places
can you imagine it
places you would have to queue up even when
you didnt *have* to queue up

the difference is back then it was worth it

        your message comes through

          is that falafal place still doing
          business that one we went to
          before i got the bus back rem
          ember

my reply

i dont know i cant get into town atm

went to morissons the other day
queue wis fucking huge
they had no plain flour
wtf

        days later and
        im still waiting
        for your reply

the wee curry shop

promises of *new normals* fall
on deaf ears for those of us who have already been
though new normal after new normal after new normal
and anyway how do they know what *normal* really is
who are they to decide to make a new version of it

when the first new normal i remember was being
the funny kid at school and then that got replaced
by a new normal of *half-breeds like you* and *takeaway boy*
and even when that new normal transmogrified
into a more self-aware new normal
back when i made my first facebook account and called
myself *noodles* or when i agreed to go on dates with people
who had *i <3 asians* in their myspace bios
it was a new normal that i wasnt entirely comfortable with

but now they promise another new normal for me
even though the last time i felt newly normal
in any unified kind of way
was sitting in the wee curry shop on buccleuch street
ordering from the set lunch-time menu
and when the pakora came the couple sitting on the table adjacent
said *those look good* and i said back *they really are*
and i asked them if they wanted to try one
an offer they politely declined
and which afterwards outside the restaurant i felt stupid for
thinking that it hadnt been my food to offer them in the first place
even if at the time it had seemed like the most natural thing to do

wing rush

the sound of helicopters above becomes overwhelmingly
present in the street as i walk down towards the park
on my allocated one-outside-walk-per-day but i start to think
what if they know my secret – that i was out in the communal
garden behind my tenement earlier i mean all i did was sit there
between the bins thinking about food or something else
non-essential but does that still count as a going out
what if the helicopter is filled with officials with telescopes
monitoring how often people go out what if people are
no longer allowed in the communal gardens behind their tenements
what if its some new government thing i havent heard about
something declared during the time it took me from leaving
my front door to this street here so devoid of people but still littered
with polystyrene containers almost as if that was all that was left of us

bloc

council tax payments are due in 10 monthly instalments from April to January however should your financial circumstances be impacted by the ongoing coronavirus outbreak it is now possible to pay by direct debit in 10 monthly instalments from 28 June 2020 to 28 March 2021 to arrange this please select the set up a direct debit option at the appropriate web address direct debit is the easiest and most cost effective way of paying council tax but if you cannot pay this way you can use the enquiry form on the same web page and select the *i am unable to pay my bill* option from the first drop down menu followed by the *i wish to defer my instalments to June* option from the second drop down and let us know you wish to move your instalments to start in June for this year a new bill will be issued before the June instalment is due 2021/22 payments will revert to the April to January monthly scheme for further information please refer to the appropriate web address below

dreams from kitchens

where is the tree my 公公 drew

after he died i received a collection of his drawings
and there it was

        the tree

he had doodled it at some point probably sitting idly
in his chair watching the weather or east
enders or listening to his cassette tapes
of cantonese opera

        the tree

perhaps it was inspired from something
he was watching or listening to at the time
perhaps it was a news report
which showed a park or the countryside
or maybe something happened in eastenders
in the park in the middle of the square there

        the tree

or maybe it was based on a tree he could see
outside from his chair – one of the overgrowing
things from the neighbours place or a tree
which used to be there years ago
before the asda got built in its place
or it could have been from an advert on the side
of the number 40 or number 40a at some point
when one of them drove by

the tree

was it from a memory he held dear – from his childhood
in the hongkong countryside – before the war split
that image apart forever – or from his first step onto
mainland british soil – there must be some trees somewhere
in liverpool – or manchester or bradford or leeds
or york or hartlepool or grimsby or somewhere he had
lived – maybe there had been a park that had held some
special meaning to him – near to the first house he bought
or the first business he opened or his wedding
or outside as he held one of his children for the first
time or even one of his grandchildren

the tree

or could it have been a representation of the tree by the burial
plot he had acquired

the one on the slight slope facing eastwards
at the bend of the small foresty path
at the south end of the cemetery

the same place where i stood that day
when i said goodbye   and then
received his drawings

lanzhou noodle

the thing about places where you can see into the cooking
area / kitchen is that you really can see it all – the amount
of physical effort that every single movement and dish requires
the gravity of a cleaver falling precisely along with the movement
of a hand – the tensing of fingers / eyes when kneading
dough – the steam rising from a pan filled with you-cant-tell
-what – i want to know what strong feelings it evokes in you to watch
your food being made rather than have it appear from a distant corner
could it be a nostalgia for something / a yearning / hunger for conn
ection to another space / time *** meanwhile far away in a kitchen
on the other side of the world a small boy watches with huge
disbelieving eyes as his grandfather quickly slices noodles
out of dough before flicking them up into the biggest pan
the boy will ever see – he knows too that its almost time

byblos cafe

my first time having fatayer was with you
you were the one who brought it up
you asked if i had ever tried *lebanese* pizza
and i said *what*

my fatayer came with spinach on top which i loved
yours had bits of some kind of cheese – honestly
they were nothing like pizza except for the part of it
which was a dough topped with things

> suddenly a memory is evoked
> of pizza eaten on the other side of the world
> the burning smell of durian atop
> a thick layer of yellow plastic melt
> an italian flag outside the entrance still entangled
> from recent typhoon winds

it was beautiful and the next night we went back again
and then again

i will never forget how
as we left into the chill drizzle that last evening above us
a neon sign glowed and i swear the word *authentic* in
authentic lebanese cuisine flickered or winked although
then again it could have just been a trick of the light

china sea

to my 公公 hongkong always seemed to be a place
of snake restaurants and poverty
violence and dismantlement
black and white photographs of unsmiling families
in stone-built courtyards

i saw him once watch
the chow yun-fat film *hong kong 1941* [1984] and cry –
saying things like *thats it*
                              yes thats it

so when other people i meet at universities or poetry
readings say that they are from hongkong and they tell me what
its like from their perspective things seem unrecognisable
even though i do recognise the place names
both from his stories
and my own limited experience

on one of my experience trips there i found myself
visiting aunties in sai kung and walking by the seafront
thinking *is this really hongkong* or eating
in a japanese restaurant on my way to doing the touristy thing
and getting the bus across the island to repulse bay
thinking *is this really hongkong* or being hassled
for money by men on nathan road thinking *is this really hongkong*

and now here i am and im really not in hongkong
but i am in a restaurant eating special fried rice [*the hoose
fried isnae worth it jist git the special* im told] and there is
a giant plastic dragon hanging over me on the ceiling
and im thinking of beautiful clear water and tourist buses
a world or two away
wondering how it could be possible for me
to have washed up this far

nandos

i cant help it – i was raised stealing sauces you see
condiments are simply too easy to slip into a bag
when nobody is looking plus the people who work
here dont give a fuck i should know ive worked
in similar places before and havent given a fuck so
why would they be any different i mean its
just a job after all its not like the few bottles of sauce
that i take from these places
will make any difference to anyone

***

plus its not like we will come back here again
we have too much pride for that

***

what do you mean
you still dont get it

its just how i was raised
theres no deeper meaning than that

fusion palace

the one internet argument ive ever involved myself in was on a forum about restaurants when i saw that someone had asked about places to get proper dim sum in glaschu as they were craving xiaolongbao and i made what i considered to be a totally helpful comment about how if its just bao you want then you have lots of options whereas if its the proper full dim sum experience instead well then youre much more limited and then someone else replied to me saying that xiaolongbao is dim sum and i wrote back and said yes but so are lots of things and the op was unclear as to whether they were enquiring about just xiaolongbao or a variety of dim sum options and then someone else posted an unrelated comment about how everyone should avoid chinese places anyway because they all have the virus and normally i try not to get involved in online fights especially when its just blatantly racist stuff i mean whats the point but when i saw that comment something in me just snapped and i began to furiously type a huge paragraph in response which cited various sources about how there was zero proof that chinese restaurants were any more unsanitary than any other places and i also made the point that the people who work and cook in these restaurants are fucking scottish man i mean they live in fucking scotland jesus christ they pay their council tax here just like anyone else but anyway in the end i deleted that entire paragraph and instead just replied with a simple fuck off which actually received more positive reactions than the racist comment which just goes to prove that i was in the right and anyway if its proper dim sum in glaschu you want then the fusion palace has a surprisingly good takeaway selection they even do duck tongues which are my favourite

loon fung

Loon

means dragon which is what describes us
because we control storms and have toes
that fall off the further east we get and even
if you beat us down in the street
shout profanities at us when we sneeze
blame pandemics on us and our eyes
we will not disappear into myth or art
we will not allow you to extinct our bodies
we will not hide behind imaginary waterfalls
dont mistake our lack of wings for an inability
to fly or belong in multiple places at once
just because we dont cough fire like you think
we should dont think that we cant fight back
dont take our silence as a muteness

fung

means phoenix which is what describes us
because we control the skies and have toes
that grasp and kill snakes and even
if you spit at us in the street
shout curses at us when we sneeze
blame a lack of progress on us and our bird brains
we will not disappear into the background
we will not allow you to say that we dont exist
we will not hide away behind imaginary firewalls
dont mistake our long wings for an inability
to hold protest signs or belong in multiple places
at once just because you cant see us
dont think that we cant see you
and that we really dont like what we see

yabbadabbadoo

your tombstone is simpler than the other
chinese ones in the anglican cemetery – no fancy
vertical calligraphy to go alongside the english
detailing age of death or words like
beloved – a photographic inlay
depicting you as you were in your 70s
– a couple decades ago now but still living

just down the road in your old house near asda
– around the time when i was still small enough
to sit with you on your chair with the tv on loud

watching fred flintstone slide down a diplodocus tail
break into a huge smile – shout his catchphrase
 which we would always join in with
– yabbadabbadooooooooooooooooooooo
i had never heard you speak english like that before

how did you do it
            sometimes i wonder how much of the tv we watched back
            then you really understood and how much of it
            was just you copying the sounds that i reacted to most
does it matter

we laughed so much that your fake teeth fell out
and i thought that was the coolest thing ever

            you were buried with them i was told
            just in case you would need them in the next world

*
*
*

eventually in the cemetery its my turn
to pay my respects and i get told to light
three incense sticks then bow three times while saying a prayer

as i do my bows i dont feel like i have enough chinese
in my vocabulary to do the prayer properly

instead a different word forms in my mind

time to go

one time my 婆婆 made a whole bowl of chicken wings just for me

one time my 婆婆 told me the same story three times in a row

one time my 婆婆 asked me when i was going to get a proper job

one time my 婆婆 walked with me down the road to get fish and chips

one time my 婆婆 made my mum cry

one time my 婆婆 called me a beautiful boy

one time my 婆婆 cooked so much food for lny that she almost fell asleep at the table while eating

one time my 婆婆 found out she had stomach cancer

one time my 婆婆 read my palm and said that i would one day be rich

one time my 婆婆 gave me and my cousin extra fish maw because she knew it was our favourite

one time my 婆婆 had a fall and broke a bone

one time my 婆婆 carried me to bed because i was sick

one time my 婆婆 asked if i wanted an orange and then told me to get her one as well

one time my 婆婆 said something racist and it changed how i looked at her

one time my 婆婆 played a two-player board game by herself to keep her mind active

one time my 婆婆 said she was old now and that she was ready to die

one time my 婆婆 asked me when i was going to finally get married

one time my 婆婆 told me to cook her a pizza since she couldnt read the english on the box

one time my 婆婆 forgave me when i said i was going to spend a week with friends instead of her one time my 婆婆 flicked through photo albums and put names to unsmiling black-and-white faces

one time my 婆婆 suggested that i call her more often

one time my 婆婆 talked to the portrait of my 公公 about if it was her time to go yet

one time my 婆婆 watched the same movie twice in a row without realising they were the same

one time my 婆婆 took me shopping for shoes because mine were falling apart

one time my 婆婆 told me to get my hair cut

one time my 婆婆 complained about everyone being on their phones

one time my 婆婆 beat me at a board game and laughed a lot

one time my 婆婆 told me stories about life in the villages of sai kung

one time my 婆婆 asked me to fix her tv for her

one time my 婆婆 gave me money for no reason

one time my 婆婆 cried

one time my 婆婆 let me go to town by myself but only if i was back by six

one time my 婆婆 bought me a rice cooker after i mentioned i didnt have one

one time my 婆婆 asked me when i could come see her again

one time my 婆婆 spent a week in the hospital and had me worried sick

one time my 婆婆 sent me home with two packs of dried sausages and a huge root of ginger

one time my 婆婆 told me off for going to the cemetery at an unlucky time of day

one time my 婆婆 hugged me and it finally hit me that she really was getting older

one time my 婆婆 said that happiness was the most important thing in life

one time i told my 婆婆 that i love her a lot

one time my 婆婆 said back that she loves me more

ACKNOWLEDGEMENTS

Huge thanks to Stuart Bartholomew and the rest of the Verve team, whose faith in my work and support are the reason this book exists. Gratitude must also go to Karlie Wu 胡嘉瑤 for the beautiful cover photo, as well as everyone at the Scottish BAME Writers Network, who kept me sane during some difficult times. Lastly, thanks to Zoe, Angie and Deborah, my companions on so many of the gastronomic adventures which inspired the writing of these poems.

An early version of "stay inside" was published on *pendemic.ie* in March 2020
"conversations from the line outside the supermarket" was first published in *Potluck Zine* Issue 1
"where is the tree my 公公 drew" was first published in *bathmagg* Issue 4

ABOUT VERVE POETRY PRESS

Verve Poetry Press is a quite new and already award-winning press that focused initially on meeting a local need in Birmingham - a need for the vibrant poetry scene here in Brum to find a way to present itself to the poetry world via publication. Co-founded by Stuart Bartholomew and Amerah Saleh, it now publishes poets from all corners of the UK - poets that speak to the city's varied and energetic qualities and will contribute to its many poetic stories.

Added to this is a colourful pamphlet series, many featuring poets who have performed at our sister festival - and a poetry show series which captures the magic of longer poetry performance pieces by festival alumni such as Polarbear, Matt Abbott and Geraldine Carver.

In 2019 the press was voted Most Innovative Publisher at the Saboteur Awards, and won the Publisher's Award for Poetry Pamphlets at the Michael Marks Awards.

Like the festival, we strive to think about poetry in inclusive ways and embrace the multiplicity of approaches towards this glorious art.

www.vervepoetrypress.com
@VervePoetryPres
mail@vervepoetrypress.com